ANCIENT GREECE

LOVERANCE
and
WOOD

TED SMART

Acknowledgements

**The publishers would like to thank Bill Le Fever, who illustrated
the see-through pages and jacket for this book, and the organizations
which have given their permission to reproduce the following pictures:**

Ronald Sheridan/Ancient Art and Architecture Collection 4, 6, 9,
21 (top left/above), 34 (top left), 40 (top left and bottom left), 42, 45
Ashmolean Museum 21 (top left/below)
Bibliothèque Nationale 30 (top left)
British Museum 7 (bottom right), 8, 11 (top right), 12 (top left), 14,
16 (top left and bottom left)), 20, 26, 28 (bottom left), 30 (bottom left), 39
C M Dixon 7 (top right), 10, 18, 19, 27 (top right),
28 (top left), 32, 35, 36 (bottom left), 44
Sonia Halliday Photographs 21 (top right)
Michael Holford 11 (bottom right), 12 (top right), 31, 34 (bottom left)
Metropolitan Museum of Art, Walter C Baker Gift Fund, 1956 15
National Archaeological Museum, Greece 27 (bottom right)
Staatliche Museum, Berlin/Ingrid Geske 36 (top right)

Illustrators:
Nigel Longden: 4, 8, 10-11, 12, 13, 14, 15, 19 (lower right),
22, 23, 26, 27, 32
Bill Le Fever: 6-7, 17, 20-21, 22 (top left and right),
24, 25, 33, 36 (top left), 37, 41
Philip Hood: 31, 34-35, 38-39, 43
Finbarr O'Connor: 18, 19 (top left), 28-29, 42
Kevin Maddison: 5, 9, 44
Richard Hook: 46-47

Editor: Julia Gorton
Series designer: Nick Leggett
Picture researcher: Ann Pestell
Production controller: Linda Spillane

This edition first published in 1995 for The Book People,
Guardian House, Borough Road, Godalming, Surrey GU7 2AE by
Hamlyn Children's Books, an imprint of Reed Children's Books,
Michelin House, 81 Fulham Road, London SW3 6RB,
and Auckland, Melbourne, Singapore and Toronto.

ISBN 1-856-13894-1

British Library Cataloguing-in-Publication Data.
A catalogue record for this book is available from the British Library.

Books printed and bound in Belgium

CONTENTS

I f we went back in time to ancient Greece, how far back would we have to go? Who were the Greeks? Where did they come from and at what point did they appear in history?

GREECE BEFORE THE GREEKS

People have lived in the Greek peninsula since the Stone Age. A skull dating from about 25000 BC was found recently in a cave in Northern Greece. In the thousands of years which followed, people learnt to domesticate animals, cultivate crops, make pots of clay and, eventually, fashion tools and weapons in bronze.

A LOST CIVILIZATION

For over a thousand years from about 3000 BC, the largest Greek island, Crete, was the most important part of the Greek world. Its people are known to us today as the Minoans, after their legendary king, Minos, who lived in a great palace at Knossos. The palace was like a small town; inside there were many comfortable houses, with beautifully decorated walls and skilful plumbing.

In about 1450 BC, a catastrophic volcanic eruption destroyed the Minoan civilization. This sudden disappearance may have been the basis for later Greek tales of Atlantis, the lost continent that sank into the sea. Apart from this myth, however, the Greeks had no memory of these earlier peoples.

THE FIRST GREEK-SPEAKERS

A new group of people arrived in Greece from central Europe around 2000 BC. They spoke Greek; or at least we know that they wrote it, rather clumsily, by drawing pictures for words, or parts of words, like Egyptian hieroglyphs. But it is still recognizably the language spoken by Greeks today, making it the oldest living European language. In the rest of the world, only Chinese has a longer history.

These first Greek-speaking peoples are known as the Mycenaeans, after one of their cities, Mycenae, on the Greek mainland. These people dominated all the lands around the Aegean Sea up until about 1100 BC. But then their influence too began to fade. This may have been because of invasion by the Dorians, a group of Greek-speaking people from the north. The Mycenaeans may also have suffered economic troubles, perhaps a series of bad harvests. Whatever the reason, they disappeared, and the Dark Ages began - a 400-year period of Greek history about which very little is known.

The Minoans built several large palaces. The largest and most impressive was at Knossos. It was five storeys high and had more than 1,300 rooms.

TALES OF OLD

One thing we do know happened during this period was that the Greeks started to use an alphabet, rather than a 'picture script', for writing. This meant that stories of the old days could be written down, instead of being passed from one generation to the next by the spoken word. Two of the most famous of these - Homer's *Iliad* and the *Odyssey* - are based on the Mycenaeans' ten-year war against Troy. Greeks in later times learnt to recite the whole of these long poems from memory.

This marble figure holding a cup, made on the islands of the Cyclades and one of the earliest pieces of Greek art, is over 4,000 years old.

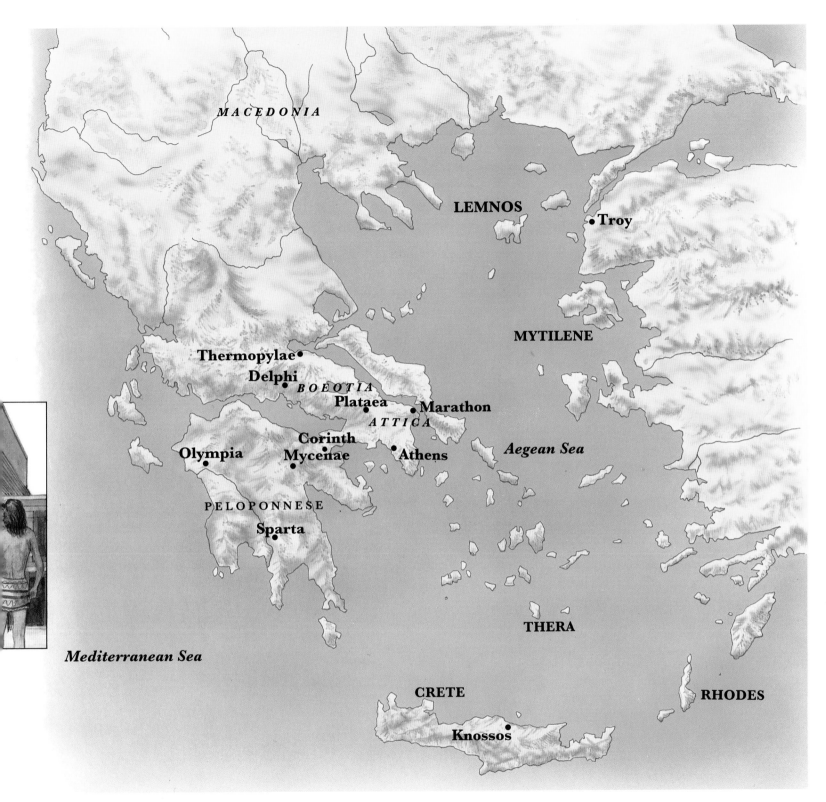

The map shows the Aegean region with the following labeled locations:

MACEDONIA

LEMNOS

Troy

MYTILENE

Thermopylae
Delphi
BOEOTIA
Plataea
Marathon
ATTICA
Corinth
Olympia
Mycenae
Athens

Aegean Sea

PELOPONNESE

Sparta

THERA

Mediterranean Sea

CRETE

RHODES

Knossos

EMERGENCE OF THE GREEKS

When Greece emerged from the Dark Ages, no one place was more important than another, as Knossos or Mycenae had been. Each area or city was independent. But all Greeks thought of themselves as one people. They called themselves Hellenes, and their country Hellas, names which they still use today. Greece is a name which was given to the country by the Romans. For the Greeks, to be a Hellene was to be 'of the same stock and the same speech', and, as the ancient Greek historian Herodotus wrote, 'to worship the same gods and keep the same customs.' What it really meant to be Greek, in life and thought, is the subject of this book.

The mainland of Greece is very mountainous. The first, scattered communities grew up in those areas where the land was fertile. The difficult terrain encouraged the growth of sea transport, which helped the Greeks spread over the eastern Mediterranean.

5

THE LAND OF GREECE

This Omphalos stone, which stood at Delphi, marked the place which was believed to be the centre of the world.

For much of the year, Greece is hot and dry. Winters, though, are often severe, and the Greeks in ancient times found it hard to earn a living from the land.

A SKELETON OF A LAND

Greece is a land of high mountains. These were once covered with trees, but, as the population grew, the forests were cut down and the good soil washed away.

There is some flat land at the foot of the mountains, but only enough to support small communities. In ancient times, the people who lived there needed all this land for growing crops, so they kept few cattle.

Some farmers spread their farms up into the hills by building terraces along the slopes. Bee-keeping was widespread amongst these people, since honey was the only sweetener known in the ancient world.

'What now remains...
is like the bones of a body
wasted and diseased, with all the
rich and fertile earth fallen away
and only the scraggy skeleton of the
land left and the mountains
supporting nothing but bees.'

— *Plato* —

A HARDY PEOPLE

The land itself had its own natural riches: fine marble for building, good clay for pottery, and some minerals - the silver mines near Athens and the iron mines of Sparta brought wealth to both these cities. But for most ancient Greeks, life was difficult and they developed into a hardy race of people as a result. The warm climate, though, gave them one great blessing; most of their daily lives could be spent in the open air.

The Greek communities that eventually grew up throughout the country were cut off from each other by high mountains. For this reason, each group had a strong sense of its own independence. We now call these groups city-states, although they were more like small towns. Fierce rivalry between the various city-states, particularly Athens and Sparta, is a key issue in Greek history.

NATURAL DEFENCES

Today, it is possible for travellers to drive through the mountains of Greece, using narrow, winding roads with many hairpin bends. In ancient times, however, the high ground could be crossed only on foot, and then with difficulty.

As natural barriers to the easy movement of people, the mountains have often played a crucial part in Greek history. This has not always worked in favour of the Greek people themselves. One important battle against the Persians, fought at a mountain pass called Thermopylae, 'the hot gates' (see pages 42 to 43), ended in defeat because the Persians discovered another way through the mountains that the Greeks thought was a secret known only to themselves.

A LANDSCAPE FOR GODS

The Greeks themselves were impressed by their remarkable landscape. They believed that the gods lived on top of their highest mountain, Mount Olympus, (2,917 m). They built their temples in sites often chosen for their natural beauty, and many of their gods were associated with the natural world - gods of rivers and trees, gods of the vine, and gods of the weather. They believed that thunder and lightning were the weapons of Zeus, greatest of all the gods.

A RECORD OF THE PAST

Away from cities like Athens, the landscape of Greece has not changed much over the centuries and we can still learn a lot about ancient Greece from it. Many sites are now being excavated and, in the country areas, much can be learnt just by walking over the land. Special techniques have even enabled archaeologists to examine old bone and pollen samples, giving us clues about the kinds of animals and plants that were common in this period of history.

This bronze figure was made in about 500 BC. It shows Zeus, father of all the gods and lord of heaven, about to throw a thunderbolt to show his displeasure with mortals.

The sanctuary of Delphi, believed to be the holiest place in Greece, was built high up on a mountainside under the cliffs of Parnassos. Pilgrims went there to learn about the future by consulting the oracle in the Temple of Apollo. They went in procession to the Great Altar to make sacrifices and say prayers before going inside.

An amphora dating from about 520 BC. It shows a group of farmers harvesting olives, using long sticks to knock down the fruits. Heavy stone presses were then used to squeeze out the oil.

THE GREEKS AND THE SEA

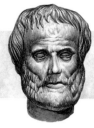

Poseidon, the brother of Zeus. His dual importance as god of both the sea and horses is shown by the shape of the mythical beast he rides.

Sea trade was vital to Athens. Ships left the port of Piraeus loaded with olive oil and silver, and sailed all over the Mediterranean. They brought back wheat, copper, iron, pitch, timber and slaves.

Greece is a country of peninsulas and islands. Ships have therefore always been a key means of transport for the Greek people and their goods. Even on the mountainous mainland, it was often easier to sail from one part to another rather than go by land.

LIKE FROGS AROUND A POND
During the Dark Ages, Greeks had already started to sail from their own small country in search of more land or wealth overseas. This search took them east to the coast of Turkey (then known as Asia Minor), north to the remote corners of the Black Sea, south to the coast of Libya, west to Italy, and even as far as southern France and Spain.

In all these places, new colonies grew up - Naples, Nice, Monaco and Marseilles were all originally founded by Greeks. Greek colonies were independent city-states, although they still remained closely linked with their home city. This was how Greek ideas and influence spread around the whole of the Mediterranean region. The philosopher Plato said that the Greeks lived around their sea like frogs around a pond.

This bronze figure, made in about 520 BC, shows a boy riding a dolphin. Aquatic subjects, such as the octopus, shell and dolphin, were popular themes in Greek art.

HEROES OF THE SEA

The Greeks constantly told each other stories about the sea. In Homer's *Odyssey*, the sea is almost the main character, battling against the hero, Odysseus, in his efforts to return home to the island of Ithaca after the Trojan War. Other stories reflect how far the Greeks ventured from their homeland; the story of Jason and the Argonauts tells of a journey to the far shores of the Black Sea in search of the Golden Fleece (the wool of a golden ram).

UNDERWATER TREASURE

In recent years, some wonderful objects have been discovered in the seas around Greece. Life-size bronze statues have been found and raised to the surface, some with eyes of coral still in place. The wrecks of whole ships, with their hundreds of amphorae (large pottery jars which once contained wine or olive oil), have been excavated by divers. The remains of over 10,000 almonds were discovered on one wrecksite, possibly harvested in Cyprus in about 300 BC. In fact, underwater archaeology has now become a specialist science, and will no doubt reveal further secrets of the past as exploration of the sea bed continues.

SEA TRAFFIC

The sea began to carry more and more trade as goods not available in Greece itself were shipped home. Few ancient cities could live on their own resources; Athens imported corn from the Black Sea, for example, in exchange for its olives and wine. More exotic imports included spices from Egypt, as well as slaves from many different countries.

There was also a trade in, and an exchange of, ideas as Greeks came into contact with other peoples. Although a very inventive people themselves, they were quick to see the value of the alphabet of the Phoenicians, the mathematics of the Babylonians, and the exquisite sculpture of the Egyptians - ideas which they 'borrowed' to enrich their own culture.

GODS OF THE SEA

The Greeks had learnt to treat the sea with respect. Sometimes it seemed a familiar place, full of fish and playful dolphins, but it could change in a moment to a strange, forbidding realm, the home of terrifying monsters and fearsome gods. One minor sea god, Nereus, was said to appear sometimes in human form and sometimes as a sea serpent. Presiding over the whole wonderful world was the god Poseidon; people believed that when he was carried along in his horse-drawn chariot, the entire earth quaked.

There were Greek colonies in many places around the coasts of Europe, North Africa and the Black Sea. The colonies had strong trading links with the rest of the Greek world. Some, such as Byzantium, became more powerful than their home city-states.

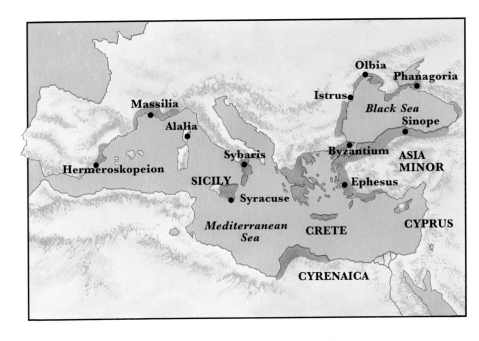

9

THE GREEK PEOPLE

Marble statues, such as this one sculpted in about 480 BC, showed perfect human forms rather than real people.

The busy, bustling agora *rang with the sound of gossip, farmers, craftworkers and merchants crying their wares, customers haggling, pigs grunting and hens cackling.*

What did the ancient Greeks really look like? The many statues that have survived from that time usually represent ideal human forms - how the sculptors thought people *ought* to look. The people shown in vase paintings are probably more realistic. However, the best clues on the true appearance of ancient Greeks have come from the bodies which have been excavated. From these, we know that they probably looked much like modern Greeks do today, often short and stocky, with dark hair and dark eyes.

A LONG LIFE

Greeks led an active life, spending a lot of their time in the open air; probably as a result of this, many of them were long-lived. Among the most famous Athenians of the fifth century BC, the soldier and writer Xenophon was 76 when he died, the playwright Aeschylus, 71, and the philosopher Plato, 82. Although we only know the exact ages of famous people, it seems likely that ordinary Greeks were long-lived as well.

THE ROLE OF WOMEN

From historical records, it would seem that the only Greeks who mattered were men, for it was only they who took part in public life. Women stayed at home, only going out occasionally, perhaps for a visit to the theatre. Women could, however, become priestesses in ancient Greece, something which they are not allowed to do in most religions today. But for the Athenians at least, the ideal woman was never mentioned at all.

As real women had such a limited real-life role, it seems strange that many classic Greek plays portray strong-willed and courageous heroines. Queen Clytemnestra, for example, murders her husband Agamemnon, the king of Mycenae, and Medea helps Jason and the Argonauts capture the Golden Fleece. Perhaps these characters represent male fears of the hidden capabilities and potential power of their womenfolk.

FOREIGNERS OR GUESTS?

Another group of people that were not allowed to take part in public life were 'foreigners', often other Greeks who had left their own city in search of work. There were about 10,000 foreigners in Athens, compared to about 40,000 Athenian 'free' men, or 'citizens'. But life was not too difficult for them; the Greek word for foreigner (*xenos*) is the same as the word for guest, and hospitality was, and still is, held to be a great virtue among the Greeks.

THE COST OF SLAVERY

Slavery was common in most ancient societies. The Greeks used it in moderation. Poorer people had one slave, or none; wealthy people usually had several. Slaves worked with their owners, helping the woman around the house, the farmer in the fields, the craftsman at his bench. The price of a slave varied according to his or her skill, but the average price in Athens was 175 drachmai (equivalent to about £700 today).

It appears that slaves were not, in general, badly treated; in fact, in Athens, slaves from Scythia could actually become policemen, since most Athenians did not like doing that particular job themselves. There were sad exceptions, though; the slave gangs that worked in the silver mines and stone quarries lived and worked in terrible conditions, but their suffering was largely ignored.

An Athenian pot dating from about 500 BC, showing a woman filling her water jar from the lion-headed spout at a fountain house. Two women leave with full jars and two approach with empty ones.

A negro slave boy cleaning a boot. Many slaves were born into captivity. Others were captured by slave dealers who followed behind the army ready to snap up any captives.

A LIFE WITHOUT LUXURY

In Sparta, matters were rather different. Citizens made up only a small part of the population - the majority were, in fact, slaves, called helots. A vicious circle was created in which the helots did all the manual work, while the citizens concentrated on training for war, largely so that they could keep the helots under control. In terms of comfort, the life of a Spartan citizen was not very different from the life of a helot; the citizens did without luxuries to keep themselves tough, so that they could maintain their army and suppress any helot rebellion.

Miniature wine jugs like this were presented to children who had reached their third birthday at a special children's festival, the Anthesteria, *held in Athens every year.*

T he family was the main unit of Greek society. However, each family was also part of a larger grouping, a brotherhood, and each brotherhood in its turn belonged to a tribe. This made the family part of a wide community.

THE HEAD OF THE FAMILY

The father was very much the head of the family. When a child was born, the father had to acknowledge it; if he did not, it was left out on a hillside to die. The father was allowed to disinherit a son who behaved badly towards him. He was also entitled to choose a husband for each of his daughters.

THE WIFE'S ROLE

A woman was controlled by her father before she was married and by her husband afterwards. However, as a wife, she had full charge of household affairs, and was respected if she ran her home efficiently. Probably then, as now, some men talked to their wives about business or politics. The Spartan king Leonidas, for example, once received a wax writing tablet without a message on it. He showed his wife, Gorgo, who correctly guessed that the message was scratched on the wood under the wax so that it would remain secret during its journey.

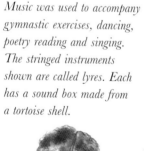

Music was used to accompany gymnastic exercises, dancing, poetry reading and singing. The stringed instruments shown are called lyres. Each has a sound box made from a tortoise shell.

This child's doll is made of terra-cotta. It was originally painted in bright colours, although most of the paint has now worn away. The doll has joints made of cord at the shoulders and knees so that its arms and legs can be moved.

CHILDREN

The children of wealthy families were often looked after by slaves, so some Greek mothers may not have had much direct contact with their sons and daughters. Perhaps for this reason, the Greeks seem to have been extremely sentimental about them. Children were a popular subject for vase-painting, and a whole range of toys, including dolls, hobby-horses and kites, were made for their entertainment. There was also a special children's festival in Athens, the *Anthesteria*, when children were crowned with flowers and given presents of miniature wine jugs.

SCHOOL DAYS

Education in Athens differed for boys and girls. Girls were educated at home, but boys between the ages of 6 and 14 went to school. The school day was long, from sunrise to sunset, and there were no long holidays. Days off were allowed for festivals, however, and there were a lot of these in some places (see pages 30 to 31).

Pupils learned reading, writing and some arithmetic. Reading was taught through the works of the epic poets. Many pupils would have been able to recite the whole of Homer's great works, the *Iliad* and the *Odyssey*. This was a great feat of memory, since the two poems had a total of 26,000 lines and reciting them aloud would have taken a full 24 hours.

Physical education was highly thought of, and training in the wrestling school was an important part of the school day. Both exercise and reciting poetry were accompanied by music, so learning to play the lyre and the double-pipes was also part of a good education.

DOING WITHOUT THE FAMILY

The Spartans were much more extreme in the way that they dealt with their children. Both boys and girls had to leave home at the age of seven to live in barracks, where all the emphasis was on physical training. They were kept hungry and encouraged to find their own food by stealing; if caught, they were beaten, not for stealing but for being found out. A famous example of model behaviour was that of the boy caught stealing a fox, who hid it under his cloak and allowed it to gnaw into his stomach rather than be found out.

In Athens, too, there was some military training; young men of 18 did two years of national service as the last stage of their education. But in Sparta, this went on for life; men could not marry until they were 30, and even then they lived in barracks rather than with their wives. In fact Sparta went further than most societies have ever done towards abolishing the family altogether.

Greek husbands did not spend much time with their families. Instead, they worked, shopped, served on juries or gossiped with their friends for most of the day.

FOOD AND FESTIVITIES

A plate decorated with fish. Fresh fish was popular but it was expensive. Poor people who could not afford it ate dried or salted fish instead.

The Greeks lived simple lives. In the warm, sunny climate, they were able to live outside most of the time. They generally wore only basic, loose-fitting clothing and survived on light meals of fresh fruit, beans and bread.

STARTING THE DAY

Breakfast was not an important meal for the Greeks. The weather was usually warm enough for them to sleep without many blankets, so they could just roll out of bed and be ready for the day. Greek clothing was very simple. Men, women, and children all wore a *chiton*, a rectangular piece of material with holes for the head and arms. Young men and children wore knee-length *chitons*; women and older men wore them rather longer, although it was considered to be showy to let a *chiton* trail on the ground. Sometimes, women also wore a *peplos*, which was similar to the chiton but open down the side and with an extra fold at the top. Outside in cold weather, both sexes added a long cloak called a *himation*.

There was plenty of wine and delicious food at a symposium. Entertainment was provided by musicians and dancing girls.

THE GREEK DIET

It was a man's job to buy food at the market; a slave would then carry the shopping home. The Greeks mainly ate bread, olives, beans and fruit. Fish was an occasional treat - although plentiful in the sea, it still had to be caught, so was considered a luxury. The ancient Greeks ate very little, if any, meat.

In Sparta, the diet was even more basic and luxuries were unheard of. One visitor, having been entertained at the public mess in Sparta, remarked, 'Now I know why the Spartans do not fear death!' When asked to name his favourite dish, a Spartan poet admitted to a craving for lentil soup, not something that many people would consider very special.

As for drink, most Greeks drank wine - coffee and tea were not drunk in Europe for another 2,000 years. The Greeks solved the problem of drunkenness by mixing wine with water. One of the reasons why Greek pots came in so many different shapes was to cater for the complicated business of storing, pouring and diluting wine to make it the right strength.

Greek tunics, called chitons, were just rectangles of linen or wool cloth draped over the body and fastened with pins or brooches at the shoulder. Young men and slaves wore short chitons - older men and women wore longer ones. A cloak called a himation was worn in the winter for extra warmth.

A DRINKING PARTY

For a special occasion, Greek food was more elaborate, and parties were very popular. Even a Spartan, the poet Alcman, wrote with excitement about a party where the tables were 'crowned with poppy-seed loaves and linseed and sesame, and among the cups, dishes of honey cake'. The party, or *symposium* as it was called, took place in the *andron*, the men's area of the house; wives and daughters would keep a safe distance.

DANCING GIRLS

A Greek party host usually employed musicians and dancing girls to amuse his guests. These girls were either slaves or unmarried women of Athenian society. Called *hetairai*, they were considered good for entertainment, but not for marriage. Wine flowed freely on these occasions, and a game called *kottabos* was played by throwing the dregs at a target. However, such parties were probably most valued for the conversations that took place.

WEDDINGS

The women of the household had their chance to take part in the festivities when there was a wedding in the family. Greek marriages were almost always arranged between families; girls were married off when they were only about 15, and they did not often meet their future husbands until the wedding day itself. Celebrations began with prayers and feasting in the bride's house; then, in the evening, the bride was escorted to the groom's home in a wedding wagon. There was no need to go to the ancient Greek equivalent of a church or a registry office; everything was done within the family circle.

A wedding procession. The bride and groom ride in a special wedding-wagon to the home of the husband.

Terra-cotta models similar to this one of a table loaded with pottery were often buried in graves with their dead owners.

This terra-cotta model shows a woman bathing. Rich people had their own bathrooms. Poor people bathed in large pots.

Most Greeks lived in the country, because that was where they worked. But whether in the country or the city, Greek houses were not luxurious. They did not have the kinds of things that we would consider essential today, such as running water, plumbing and fitted kitchens.

COOKING AND WASHING

Water in a Greek home was drawn from a well. The well could be as much as 15 m deep, so hauling water was quite a chore for the slaves. Sometimes they fetched it from the public fountains instead. Some rooms inside the house may have been set aside for a particular purpose, like cooking or washing, but they did not usually have built-in fittings. Cooking was done over a portable brazier or sometimes in a stone oven. In the bathroom, a large pot was used as a toilet, which the slaves would empty into the gutter outside. Only a few, rich people had their own drains, leading out into the street.

MULTI-PURPOSE FURNITURE

The Greeks liked to sit, or recline, on low couches and benches, and eat their food from low tables. They kept their clothing in chests, not wardrobes, since their *chitons* and other simple garments could be carefully folded up and stored flat without getting creased up.

Other furniture in a Greek house included armless chairs and couches, both with seats made of leather or fibre cords. Some pieces were used for several different purposes. A couch, for example, would serve as something to eat from, a place to relax on, and even a bed to sleep on.

> 'The house contains few elaborate decorations. The rooms are designed simply to provide a suitable setting for the things that are to fill them, and thus each room invites just what is fitting for it.'
>
> — *Xenophon*

INTERIOR DECORATION

The art of laying mosaics (pictures made from small pieces of stone or glass) was invented by the Greeks. Elaborate mosaics, though, were not often seen in private houses. Sometimes, the *andron* (men's quarters) of a rich Greek household had mosaic floors, usually made from different coloured river pebbles laid out in designs using basic shapes such as triangles, circles and squares. However, most floors in the house were simply of beaten earth.

The walls were probably just bare plaster. Sometimes, they were hung with brightly-coloured, patterned tapestries woven by the women of the house. The most splendid of these would be found in the *andron*, almost always the most elaborately decorated and painted room in a Greek house. One rich Athenian, a man called Alcibiades, had his dining room walls specially painted by a theatrical designer, showing various scenes in perspective, as might be seen on a theatre backdrop. The paintings must have been quite a talking point amongst his guests.

Less wealthy people often hung pots, pans, and other useful items on their walls. This ingeniously solved the problem of storage as well as decoration.

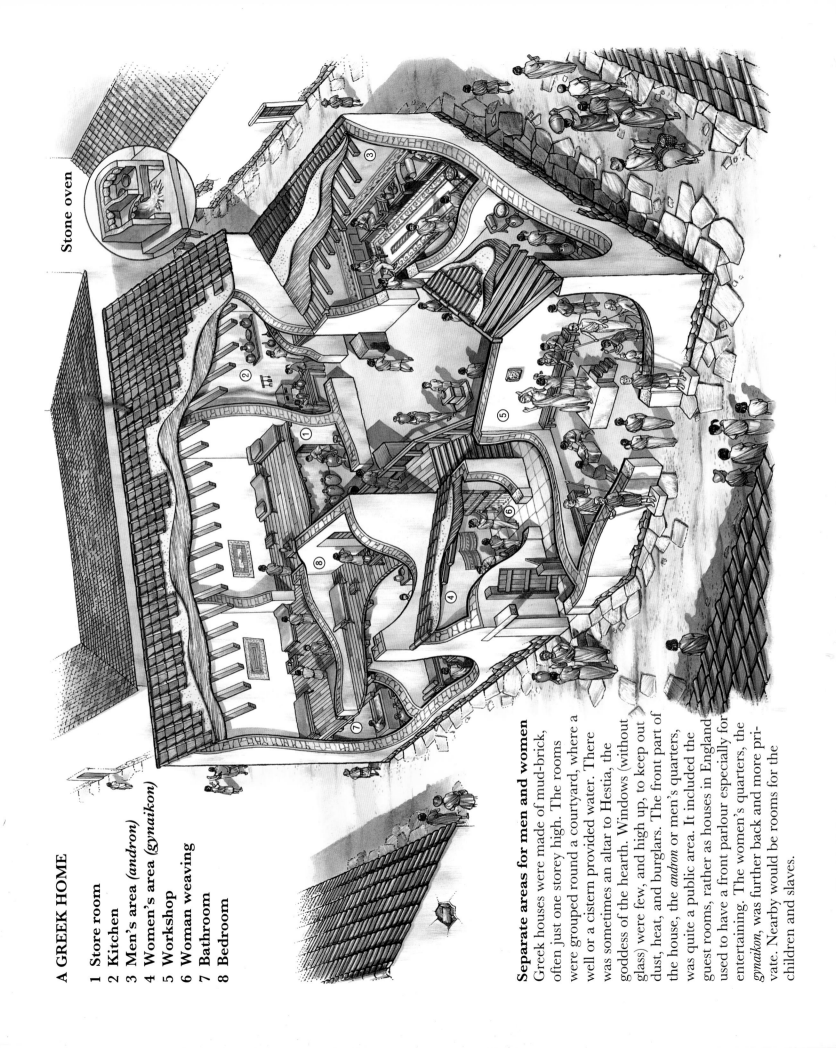

Stone oven

A GREEK HOME

1 Store room
2 Kitchen
3 Men's area (andron)
4 Women's area (gynaikon)
5 Workshop
6 Woman weaving
7 Bathroom
8 Bedroom

Separate areas for men and women

Greek houses were made of mud-brick, often just one storey high. The rooms were grouped round a courtyard, where a well or a cistern provided water. There was sometimes an altar to Hestia, the goddess of the hearth. Windows (without glass) were few, and high up, to keep out dust, heat, and burglars. The front part of the house, the *andron* or men's quarters, was quite a public area. It included the guest rooms, rather as houses in England used to have a front parlour especially for entertaining. The women's quarters, the *gynaikon*, was further back and more private. Nearby would be rooms for the children and slaves.

THE WORLD OF WORK

A terra-cotta model of a woman slave fanning a kitchen fire. Fanning made the charcoal hot enough to cook supper, the only warm meal of the day.

The Greeks - farmers, crafts-men and state officials alike - worked hard at their various occupations, always valuing a job well done, and keenly appreciating quality and craftsmanship. But most people did not live to work - other things, like being a good citizen, were often more important to them.

WOMEN AT WORK

Women had slaves to help them with domestic chores such as cooking. This left them free to spend their time weaving cloth; clothes, curtains, and cushion-covers were all produced within the home.

A whole range of equipment was needed for weaving. Wool or flax was used to make the cloth; cotton was then very rare. First, the wool or flax was washed, combed and dyed. Most of the dyes used were made from earth and plants, although one, a brilliant purple, came from a kind of shellfish. Next, the wool or flax was spun into thread by hand with a distaff and spindle - the spinning-wheel had not then been invented. Finally, the thread was woven into cloth on a vertical loom held down with special loom weights.

Sheep's wool, which was bought as a fleece, had to have the burrs removed, be washed, and then dyed. Married women wove and their daughters spun. The weather was usually good, so the work was often done in the courtyard.

THE FARMING ROUND

Farming was vitally important to the economy of ancient Greece. During the Peloponnesian War (see pages 42 to 43), the Spartan general Brasidas was able to subdue Acanthus, a neutral city, simply by threatening to destroy its fruit crop.

Many city-dwellers, as well as country folk, worked on the land. The farming year followed a regular cycle. In spring-time, the farmers and their workers pre-pared for the May grain harvest; in au-tumn, they harvested grapes and olives, as well as ploughing and resowing the fields ready for the next crop. Summer and winter were not so busy, which gave them plenty of time for other pursuits, such as war and politics.

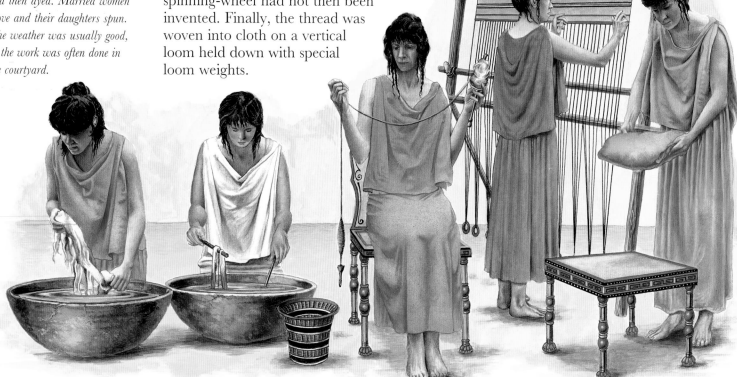

INDUSTRIALIZATION

Ancient Greek craftsmen took much personal pride in the goods they produced. One of the reasons they were able to do so was because they worked on such a small scale. Factories were almost unheard of, although we do know of one which employed 20 slaves to produce bedsteads, and another with 30 slaves who made swords. Some larger factories were set up in times of war, when the demand for weapons and armour increased, but these were still tiny by today's standards.

The only example of industrialization on a scale approaching that of modern times was in the silver mines of Lavrion in Attica. The state leased out the mining rights to rich men who then worked the mines using slave gangs. The Athenian general Nicias hired out 1,000 of his slaves to work in the silver mines, at enormous profit to himself.

The Greeks used many different tools, including hammers, axes, drills and lathes, which were made from bronze and, later, iron. This terra-cotta model shows a worker using a saw.

RICH AND POOR

As a result of this kind of exploitation, there were both very rich and very poor people in Greek society. But to help make the system a bit fairer, there was a clever method of taxing the rich, called liturgies. Rich men had to perform special services for the state, such as paying for the chorus in plays at drama festivals. Many grumbled about paying up, but at least they knew what the money was being spent on and could take pride in the quality of the service they provided.

Vines grew well on the hot Greek hillsides. Grapes were put into wicker baskets and the juice squeezed out by treading on them. Wine was mixed with water before being drunk.

LIVING OVER THE SHOP

Many different kinds of craftsmen - potters, sculptors and smiths, for example - worked in the cities. Usually, each craft was practised in one particular area of the city, and this often remained the same over a long period; one house in Athens was occupied by marble sculptors for 200 years. The main craft practised in Athens was pottery-making, with about 100 vase painters alone working in the Kerameikos, the potters' quarter.

Craftsmen sold their goods direct - there were no retailers to buy goods from suppliers and then sell them to the customers. This is why many Greeks lived as near as possible to their own shops. As a result, the only special city shopping areas were the market places.

Greeks went barefoot at home, but wore leather sandals or boots out of doors. People had these made to measure at a cobbler's workshop or a cobbler's stall in the agora.

CITY-STATES

Pericles, leader of Athens in a 'Golden Age' when the city's wealth and power was at its height, organised a building programme to beautify the city.

Ancient Greece was made up of over 100 city-states, and every Greek was a member of one of them. Their own word for city-state - *polis* - has actually given us the modern English word 'politics', meaning the art of governing a state.

TOWN AND COUNTRY

A city-state included both the city and its surrounding countryside. When Greeks talked about the Athenians, therefore, they actually meant the inhabitants of the city of Athens, and the people who lived in Attica, the area around it. The lifestyles of city-dwellers and country folk were obviously very different, so their interests were not always the same. In his sad comedy *The Acharnians*, the playwright Aristophanes tells of how much the men from one small village of Attica missed their homes when they had to seek refuge in Athens during the Peloponnesian War (see pages 42 to 43).

KNOWING EVERYONE BY SIGHT

All the adult men born in a *polis* qualified as citizens of that particular city-state. A state of 10,000 citizens would have a total population of around 100,000 (about 40,000 women, children, and foreigners and perhaps 50,000 slaves). Most city-states were small, with less than 10,000 citizens. Athens was unusually large, with about 40,000 citizens; Sparta had only 9,000 citizens, but these were heavily outnumbered by about 60,000 helots (see pages 10 to 11).

The philosopher Aristotle said that each citizen should know all the others by sight - only then could a democracy work properly. He believed that democracy was not possible in larger states of, say, 100,000 citizens and a total population of 1,000,000 people.

The ceremonial centre of Athens was the Acropolis ('high fortress'). The largest building is the Parthenon (temple of Athena). Note the 10-metre high statue of Athena nearby.

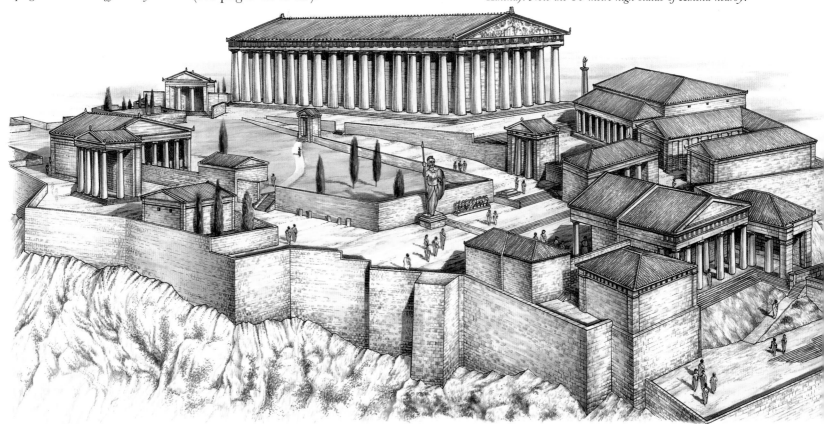

Greek coins were made of gold or silver. They were often stamped with various symbols of the issuing city-state on one side, and the head of a popular god on the other.

DIPLOMACY AND ALLIANCES

Today, countries negotiate with each other through their ambassadors, specially appointed officials who live in foreign cities and act on behalf of their homeland. In ancient Greece, however, things were different - Sparta, for example, was represented in Athens by an Athenian offical who had agreed to act in Sparta's interests.

Some cities were grouped together into special alliances. The cities of Boeotia, for example, formed the Boeotian League, and the coastal cities of the Aegean formed the Athenian Empire. Alliances were unusual, however, and often made only for a particular purpose, such as fighting against the Persians.

PROTECTIVE WALLS

Special defensive walls were built around some ancient Greek cities for protection against enemy attack. The land walls of Athens stretched from the city all the way to the port of Piraeus, about 5 km away. They were built in a great hurry, soon after the Persian Wars.

Sparta did not have any protective walls, but it was so well defended naturally that it became known as the citadel of Greece. Firstly, the sheer size of its territory meant that it was not as vulnerable to surprise attack as some of the other city-states. Also, Sparta was surrounded by the Taygetus mountain range, a formidable barrier to any would-be invader.

TIME AND MONEY

Each city-state had its own traditions and customs. Even calendars differed, which could make day-to-day arrangements between city-states, and the general dating of events, very confusing.

All city-states produced their own coins, each stamped with the symbol of that particular city. Coins were a fairly recent invention then, and there was no fixed rate of exchange; people bargained with each other until they reached an agreed deal. Some coins could only be used in their home state - others, such as the Athenian *glaukes* (showing the head of Athena on the front and an owl, her symbol, on the back), were accepted all over the Greek world.

CITY PRIDE

The city-states were very different from one another, and the Greek people often had fairly fixed ideas about the identity of each. Natives of one city-state were often rude about the people of another; Athenians referred to the farmers of neighbouring Boeotia as Boeotian pigs. Local pride was very strong, especially amongst the Spartans. The brave Spartan soldiers who died after refusing to flee from the Persians at Thermopylae, even though they were heavily outnumbered, were remembered in a famous epigram: 'Go, tell the Spartans, stranger passing by; that here, obedient to their laws we lie.'

A marble statue of a Spartan warrior. It is thought to be Leonidas, King of Sparta from about 490-480 BC, and may have come from a memorial to the Spartans killed at the battle of Thermopylae.

21

DEMOCRACY

At the end of a trial, the jury voted, using discs similar to these, to show whether they thought the accused person was guilty or not guilty.

Each juror fitted a bronze ticket with his name in a slot in an allotment 'machine'. Each day, different rows of names were chosen to serve in court.

Each city-state in Greece had its own distinctive style of government, but all were based on a love of freedom and independence. The Greeks did not want to live like their neighbours, the Persians, who were considered little more than slaves to their king.

GOVERNMENT IN SPARTA

Sparta had a peculiar system of government which seemed strange to all the other city-states. Rule was shared between two kings, five *ephors* (magistrates elected each year), a Senate, and an Assembly. The idea behind this arrangement was that no one part of the state should be allowed more power than any other.

A water clock. Speakers in court could only speak for as long as it took the water to run out of the top cup into the bottom one. Many Greek men enjoyed sitting on juries, partly because it meant a paid day off from work.

RULING SYSTEMS

Many city-states were ruled by groups of wealthy men. Each of these ruling groups was known as an oligarchy, meaning 'the rule of the few'. Some cities, like Athens, were ruled by an oligarchy only in times of difficulty; others, like Thebes, were always governed in this way.

The kind of government for which the Greeks are most remembered, however, is democracy, meaning 'the rule of the people'. Ancient Greek democracy, though, was quite different from democracy today. Because of the size of modern states, democracies are now run by a group of individuals elected to represent the people of a nation in a parliament or other assembly. Greek cities were small enough for all citizens (adult men who had been born in the city-state) to have the right to attend the assembly themselves.

People were paid for taking time off work to help run the democracy. Jury service, for example, required huge numbers of people; there were often 10 courts sitting at once, and several hundred people on each jury. The Athenians enjoyed the legal process. There were no judges, barristers, or solicitors, and people spoke in their own defence.

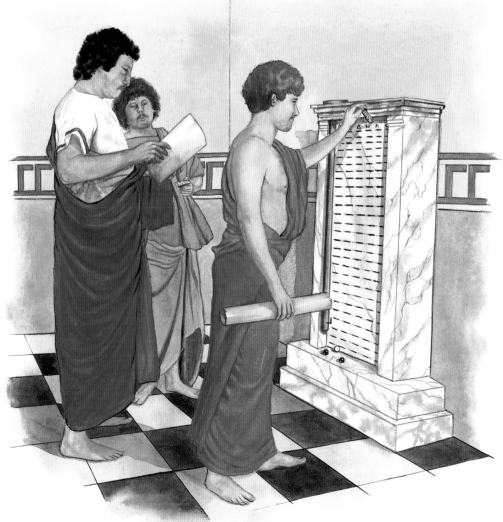

DANGERS OF A GOOD SPEAKER

Everyone had a right to speak at the assembly. However, some people were more skilled at public speaking than others, so were better able to persuade the people that their opinion was right. Once, during the Peloponnesian War, news arrived in Athens that the island of Mytilene had revolted against Athenian rule. After a heated debate, involving some clever speech-making by a few outraged citizens, the Athenian Assembly voted·to put to death or enslave everyone on the island. The next day, the Athenians were so appalled at what they had done that they called another assembly and reversed the decision. Luckily, the second order arrived at the island just in time to save the lives of the inhabitants.

Sometimes, when it was feared that one good speaker was swaying the assembly too much, the people voted to have an ostracism. Everyone was invited to write down on an *ostrakon*, a fragment of pottery, the name of any man they felt was acting wrongly. If more than 6,000 people voted, the man who got the most votes was banished from the city for 10 years.

'There is a class of people in Athens, gentlemen, who excel at voicing the rights of others in this assembly. To them my recommendation would be simply this; they should make it their aim to do justice to Athens when speaking to others. They will then begin by doing their own duty...'

— *Demosthenes* —

PLAYING ONE'S PART

In the same way that some people do not bother to vote in elections today, a few Greeks did not enjoy fulfilling their democratic responsibilities. These people were dealt with severely. Whilst an assembly was being held, a gang of slaves walked around looking for anyone who was trying to avoid going to the meeting. Each of the slaves carried a rope dipped in red paint, and anyone who was caught was daubed, an object of ridicule to other people. Offenders often had to pay a fine, as well.

Although every citizen had the chance to speak and affect decisions taken, Athenian democracy was not always fair. A single defeat in wartime or an unexpected disaster such as a plague or a famine could lead to panic and the fickle mob would turn on their leader - even one as great as Pericles. Some Athenians complained that ignorant, poor people had too much power. But most Athenians cherished their system.

PUBLIC LIFE

Official measures used to measure corn, wine, oil and other goods. They stopped any cheating and helped officials settle arguments between traders and their customers.

The splendid Athenian agora, *a large open market place where farmers and craftworkers sold their produce. Stalls were set up in the open area as well as inside the long, colonnaded buildings called* stoas.

The large, open space known as the *agora* was the central public meeting place in a Greek city. This space was carefully protected; there were boundary stones around its edge and no one was allowed to build houses or anything else on it.

POWER ON DISPLAY?

The *agora* of Athens, which was surrounded by many fine public buildings, was an impressive sight. But this was not the case in every city-state - the Spartan *agora* was particularly dull and uninteresting. The historian Thucydides said that if Sparta ever became deserted, no one visiting the city in later days would believe how powerful it had once been.

PRESIDENT FOR A DAY

Some of the buildings around the *agora* in Athens were used for the government of the city. The assembly itself, however, was so large (at least 6,000 citizens had to be present for the meeting to proceed) that it had to gather just outside the city on a hill called the Pnyx.

The assembly met about every 10 days to pass laws. The job of drafting the laws was done by the council, or *boulé*, which met in one of the agora buildings, the Bouleuterion. The *boulé* was made up of 500 men chosen by lot, 50 from each of the 10 tribes into which the citizens of Athens were divided for political purposes. The *boulé* was still very large, however, so each group of 50 served in turn to lead the council as an executive committee, the *prytany*, which met every day. Each day a new president was elected, and for that day he was head of the Athenian state and had the power to declare war. This was only allowed to happen to a man once in his lifetime.

During its period of office, the executive committee lived in the Tholos, close to the Bouleuterion. Seventeen committee members slept in the Tholos at night, so that someone was always on duty in case of emergency. Meals were provided at public expense. Fragments of pottery have been found with 'DE' scratched on them, short for *demosion* ('public'), presumably so that *prytany* members would not walk off with pieces of the official dinner service!

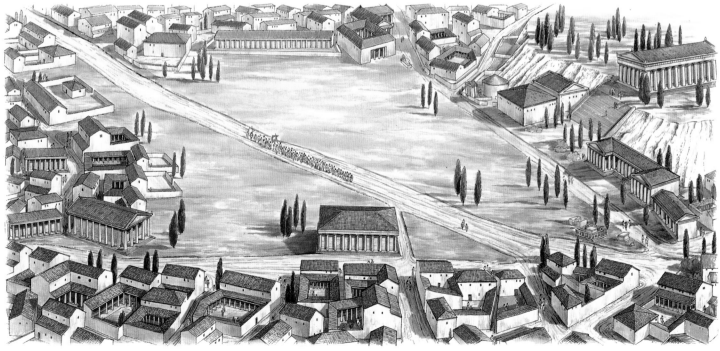

THE AGORA IN ATHENS

1 Bouleuterion (council chamber)
2 Seats for council of 500 (*boulé*)
3 Tholos
4 Beds
5 Tables for eating
6 Old Bouleuterion
7 Public records and state documents

Government buildings

These three government buildings stood at the edge of the Athenian *agora*. The Old Bouleuterion, built in about 500 BC, was the original meeting house of the council or *boulé*. It fell out of use as a debating chamber in about 400 BC, after which it was used to store public records and state documents. The *boulé* then met in the new Bouleuterion. The Tholos was an eating and sleeping place for the *prytany*. It had a kitchen and toilet at the back. The Tholos was also the place where standard weights and measures were kept. Five officials were appointed by lot to make sure that fair measures were used. They would have been kept busy, because many shopkeepers set up their stalls around the *agora*, jostling each other for the best site.

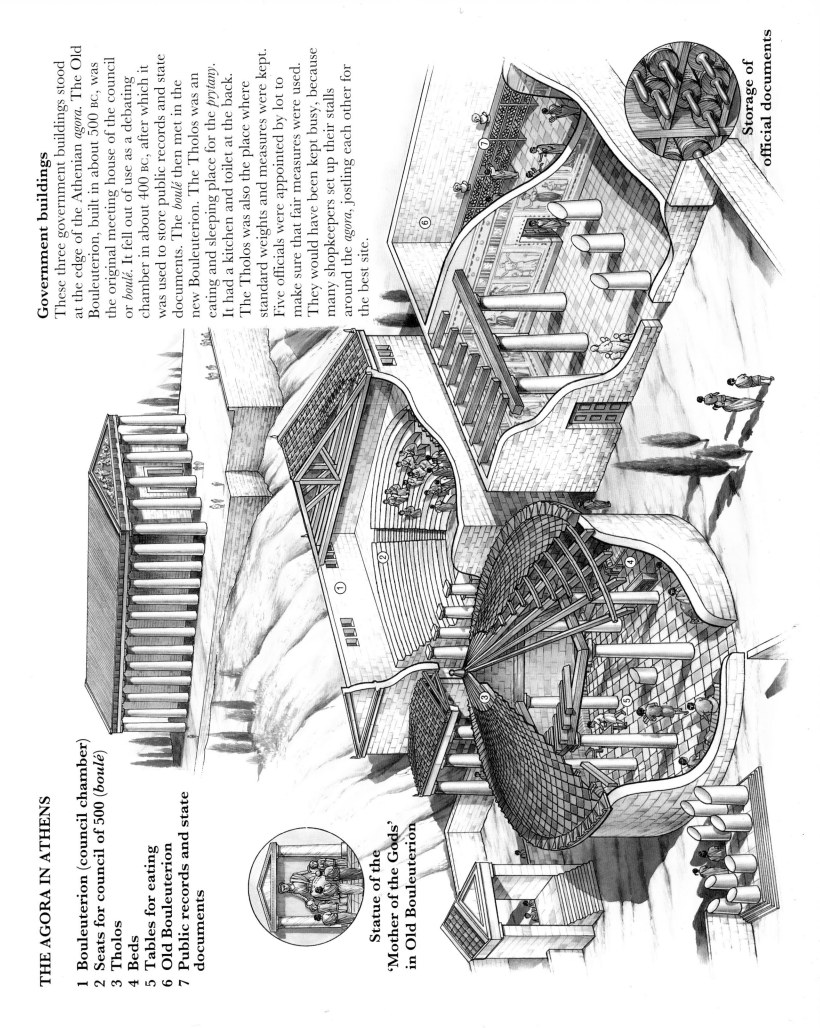

Statue of the 'Mother of the Gods' in Old Bouleuterion

Storage of official documents

SCIENCE AND PHILOSOPHY

'Votive' works, similar to this one, were commissioned by grateful patients to thank the gods for successful cures.

Many Greeks, preferring their traditional superstitions, were suspicious of philosophers, but some were keen to discuss the new ideas.

As they sheltered from the sun in the open-sided market buildings around the *agora*, the Greeks loved to talk and argue. They discussed all aspects of the world around them - the way it worked, the meaning of life, and the nature of human behaviour. They called this study philosophy, meaning 'the love of wisdom'.

OBSERVATION OR THEORY

The love of wisdom led some Greeks to the first discovery of many of the scientific laws and principles of nature. This was done through careful observation and calculation. The scientist Archimedes, for example, noticed the water level rise and fall as he got in and out of his bath. He realized that each time he got in, his body displaced its own volume of water. He went on to work out that the same would be true for any object placed in water, and gave his famous yell of excitement 'Eureka!', which means 'I've got it!'

Other Greeks wanted to go beyond pure observation and try to understand the underlying meaning of the physical world. What was the world made of? Did things really move, or only appear to move? The Greeks were fascinated by many of the same questions that physicists ask today. Some of their conclusions were wrong - some were remarkably accurate. One theory that we now accept as true was first put forward by a Greek scientist, Leucippus of Miletus. He suggested that the universe was made up of an infinite number of tiny particles, or atoms, joining up in different combinations and always moving. Modern scientific experiment has proved him correct.

This mechanical screw, devised by Archimedes to raise water from a river onto land, was one of the few contributions that the Greeks made to technology.

THE NEW MEDICINE

The same scientific approach began to be used in medicine, too. Hippocrates was one of the first doctors who did not regard illness simply as a punishment from the gods - he examined his patients to find out what was wrong with them, and tried to prescribe suitable, practical treatments. Hippocrates' ideas were surprisingly modern. He always began each treatment by finding out everything he could about the patient; age, type of work, and even behaviour and sleep patterns. This was all before he asked about the symptoms of the illness itself. Hippocrates gave his name to the Hippocratic Oath, by which doctors promised to work in the best interests of their patients. A version of the oath is still taken by doctors today.

MATHEMATICS

The Greeks also worked out some basic rules of maths for the first time. Pythagoras of Samos experimented with patterns, using pebbles in sand, until he finally worked out his famous theorem on the relative lengths of the sides of a right-angled triangle. He also realized that the notes of the scale in music are mathematically related to the length of the string being plucked, or to the length of the pipe being blown.

PUTTING SCIENCE TO USE

Although they made such an important contribution to the development of scientific knowledge, the Greeks did not show much interest in technology - putting that knowledge to practical use. For much of their history, they survived without such basic devices as the windmill. They did want to show that science should be taken seriously, however. Thales of Miletus put his knowledge of weather patterns to practical effect; foreseeing a spell of favourable weather and judging that the olive crop would be very good as a result, he bought up as many olive-presses as he could lay his hands on and earned himself a handsome profit.

THE PERILS OF THOUGHT

The qualities of curiosity and imagination of some Greeks were not always valued by others. The famous philosopher, Socrates, knew that the wisest man was the one who knew that he knew nothing. But when he tried to convince his fellow Athenians that they too knew nothing, it proved too much for them. He was condemned to death for insulting the gods and corrupting the young, and died after drinking the cup of hemlock (juice extracted from a poisonous plant) given to him as punishment.

Socrates, one of the greatest Greek thinkers, led people to the truth by asking questions and letting them answer in their own way.

In the background of this votive relief, the patient is bitten by a snake. In the foreground, the doctor treats the patient.

SPORT AND GAMES

Exercising the body was just as important to the Greeks as exercising the mind. A good citizen began to take part in sports and games during youth, and was expected to continue as long as he was physically able.

A WOMAN'S GAME

Women and girls, however, did not really have a chance to join in with sport; in Athens, the only game we know girls played together was knucklebones. This became known as a woman's game, but games of chance were clearly enjoyed by everyone. In fact, we can still see make-shift boards scratched on the marble seats of ancient Greek theatres; people must have enjoyed playing board games as they waited for the action to start.

Hockey seems to have been played only by boys. Generally, though, team games were not popular. The Greeks mainly used sport to encourage the individual to excel, particularly in athletic events.

This life-size figure of a charioteer originally stood on a chariot drawn by four horses.

Knucklebones, popular amongst women and boys, was played with the ankle-joints of goats or cows. Each one was thrown up, then caught and held on the back of the hand.

RUNNING

Probably the most popular sport of all was running. The Greeks raced against each other on sand to make it more difficult. As in modern athletics, there were different lengths of race: simple (the length of a stadium, about 200 m); double (two lengths); and the long race (sometimes as many as 24 stadia, or 4,000 m). There was one race that was run in armour - the basic purpose of all this exercise, after all, was to keep men fit to serve in the army. The especially long Marathon, a popular event today, was one race which was *not* run by the Greeks. However, it takes its name from the famous run to bring news of victory at the battle of Marathon (see pages 42 to 43) to Athens 42 km away.

WRESTLING AND BOXING

The Greeks thought highly of skill at wrestling, because the sport required a combination of strength, suppleness, and presence of mind. Wrestling contests took place in mud and dust - the dust made it easier to get a hold on one's opponent and the mud made it harder! To win, a man had to get his opponent down onto his back (so that his shoulders touched the ground) three times.

In boxing, each athlete's head was protected by a bronze cap. This was very necessary, since contestants' fists were armed with leather thonging studded with metal. The results of these contests were often bloody. Worse still was the *pancration*, a combination of wrestling and boxing, in which a man was allowed to seize and hit his opponent, and even strangle him - although biting was ruled out.

THE PENTATHLON

Contestants in the pentathlon had to take part in five different events (*penta* means five in Greek). In addition to running and wrestling, there was long jump, throwing the discus and throwing the javelin. There was no high jump contest in ancient Greek games. It is not clear what technique was used in the long jump - the distances recorded are quite large, so it may have been more like a hop, step, and jump (like today's triple jump) than modern long jump. Long jump contestants also carried stone or metal weights. These were probably swung forward as the athletes jumped to help increase their forward movement. No one is really sure how the pentathlon was judged - it seems likely that only the winners of the long jump, discus and javelin events qualified to compete in the running and wrestling.

ANIMAL SPORTS

The Greeks apparently saw nothing wrong in using animals for sport. Cocks, quails, and partridges were all used for fighting. Bets were placed on the results of the fights.

The main animal sport, popular with everyone, although only the rich could afford to take part, was chariot-racing. The prize in these events went to the owner of the horse, not to the charioteer, and this gave a rare chance for women to take part. Kyniska, sister of a Spartan king, was the first woman-owner to race horses at Olympia.

Every four years, all fighting stopped while the Olympic Games were held. The games, which were dedicated to Zeus, included chariot-racing, running, boxing and wrestling. Each winner received a simple laurel wreath.

RELIGIOUS FESTIVALS

Spartans in padded costumes dancing around a wine jar, probably as part of a ceremony connected with the worship of Dionysus, god of wine.

Part of the Parthenon frieze showing the Panathenaic festival held every four years. This heifer is about to be sacrificed to the goddess.

Because physical training was felt to be so important, the many festivals held to worship the Greek gods and goddesses always featured various athletic events, as well as processions and rites and rituals.

OLYMPIA

Some religious festivals consisted almost exclusively of athletic events. The famous competitive games held every four years at Olympia were dedicated to the god Zeus. These were panhellenic games, which means that all Greeks were allowed to take part. For the occasion, heralds were sent to proclaim a truce throughout the Greek world and all fighting stopped.

Other panhellenic games included those held at Delphi in honour of the god Apollo, at Isthmia in honour of Poseidon, and at Nemea, again in honour of Zeus. The four came to be known as a circuit, and some athletes travelled from place to place to take part in them all.

WINNING OR TAKING PART?

Local city festivals often had a sporting element, too. In Athens, for example, at the Panathenaic festival in honour of the goddess Athena, many kinds of races took place in the *agora*, including a particularly dangerous one that seems to have required jumping on and off a moving chariot. The prizes for winning here were specially commissioned vases of Athenian pottery, filled with olive oil from Attica. This was a good way of advertising the city's products. Nothing, however, compared with the glory of winning at Olympia, where the prize was simply a wreath of olive.

PROCESSIONS

The centrepiece of the Panathenaia was the procession - processions usually played an important part in most Greek festivals. Like a state occasion today, it required a lot of organization; everyone had to be in the right order, wearing the right robes and carrying the appropriate vessels and baskets. Singers and musicians were also essential. Processions like these were the best chance women had to appear in public life. The great sight at the Panathenaic procession was the new robe for the statue of Athena, which was carried like a flag attached to the mast of a ship. The women who had woven this vast robe played an important part in the procession.

SACRIFICES

The Panathenaic festival always ended with a sacrifice. Human sacrifice had been practised in Greece in earlier times, and probably still happened in Classical times in country areas. But generally an animal - either a cow, sheep or goat - was sacrificed. Some of the animal was set aside for the god, but this was usually the least appetizing parts. The rest of the animal was cooked and eaten, a rare treat for most Greeks.

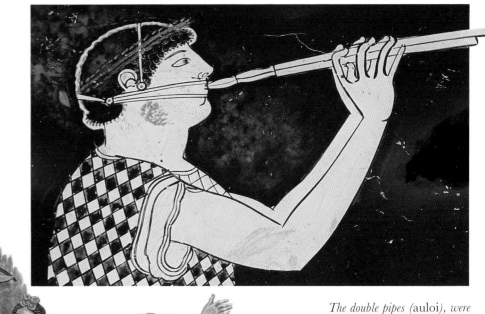

*The double pipes (*auloi*), were often played in festivals and processions. The pipes were fitted with reeds, like a modern oboe, and were held in the mouth by a leather strap.*

The climax of the Panathenaic festival was the procession carrying the new robe for the statue of Athena, housed in the Erechtheum. The robe was fastened to the mast of a ship which was pulled through the city on rollers.

POPULAR PARTIES

Even in sober Sparta, festivals were taken seriously. There was a ceremony in the spring before the ploughing started, when choirs of girls, chosen from the best families, would welcome the dawn. Despite their enthusiasm for war, the Spartans refused to turn up in time for the Battle of Marathon because they were celebrating a festival of the full moon. Athens, too, was proud of the number of festivals included in its calendar; they added up to about 150 days in a year. Ambitious parents, though, worried that their children were getting too much time off school.

THE THEATRE

Going to the theatre and going to church are today seen as very different activities. But staging plays was one of the ways that the Greeks honoured their gods. Dionysus was the god of the theatre and the god of wine, since both were seen as ways of transporting people beyond their everyday experience.

SONG AND DANCE

Drama developed from the songs and dances which were performed during the worship of Dionysus. Plays took place on a circle of flat ground called the *orchestra*, which means 'the dancing place' in Greek; originally, this was probably the area set aside for threshing corn in Greek villages.

A chorus of singers and dancers always played an important part in any Greek play. Gradually, though, their leader separated himself from them and made spoken comments - this was the beginning of acting. But there were no more than three actors, and songs and dances often took place between each scene. This would make a visit to the theatre in ancient Greece more like going to the opera today.

PLAYWRIGHTS AND PRIZES

Plays, like sports and games, were often put on competitively. Competitions in Athens sometimes went on for four days, usually with three comic and three tragic playwrights taking part. Prizes were awarded to the writers of the best plays - originally a ram for tragedy and a basket of figs and an amphora of wine for comedy. Later the successful playwrights were crowned with ivy, as if they were athletes.

'Truly to be clad in feathers is the very best of things.
Only fancy, dear spectators, had you each a brace of wings,
Never need you, tired and hungry, at a tragic chorus stay:
You would lightly, when it bored you, spread your wings and fly away,
Before returning, after luncheon, to enjoy our comic play.'

——— *Aristophanes* ———

A terra-cotta model of a comic actor playing the part of a slave. He wears a mask of stiffened linen.

Greek actors in a play. The two on the right, who are joined together by a cloak in the manner of a pantomime horse, are playing the part of a centaur called Chiron.

32

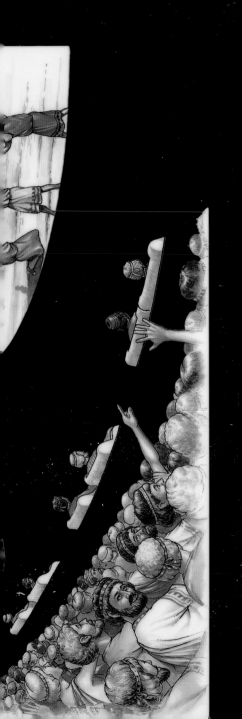

A GREEK THEATRE

1 *Orchestra*
2 *Skene*
3 Crane
4 *Proskenion*
5 Movable panel
6 Scenery
7 *Theatron*
   (audience area)
8 Judges' seats
9 Altar
10 Actors
11 Dressing room

Plan of theatre

Masked theatre

Although the first ancient Greek theatres were little more than bare hillsides, they did become more elaborate. In the open air, without stage and curtains, scene changes and lighting were very limited. Scenery was painted canvas hung on the wooden stage building, or *skene*. The action took place in the circular *orchestra*, or on a platform in front of the *skene* called the *proskenion*. There were no women actors; men played women's roles. This was one reason why everyone wore masks, which also helped project the actors' voices to the audience.

GODS AND GODDESSES

Dionysus, god of wine, making a vine grow from the deck of his ship and turning his pirate kidnappers into dolphins.

It was clear to the Greeks that no matter how much a man loved his children, went regularly to the *gymnasium,* and was active in the political life of his city, he was still not in control of events. There were unseen forces at work, which the Greeks called *moira*, or fate, and no one could really foresee what the future had in store.

THE OLYMPIANS

The Greeks believed in the existence of various gods and goddesses who had power over fate. They therefore aimed to keep the gods happy to ensure future good fortune and success. All the most important activities in the Greek world - games, theatrical events, processions, and sacrifices - were dedicated to one god or another, depending on local custom.

Many different gods and goddesses were worshipped throughout Greece, but there were 12 particularly important ones. These gods lived on Mount Olympus, the highest mountain in Greece. Their special diet of nectar and ambrosia stopped them from growing old and dying.

The most powerful of the 12 Olympian gods was Zeus. His brother Poseidon was ruler of the seas, and his son, Apollo, who was worshipped at Delphi, was the god of music. Hephaestus was the smith god and Ares was the god of war, although he was not as important as his title might suggest. Hermes, with his winged sandals, was the gods' messenger.

Among the goddesses, Hera, Zeus' wife, was the goddess of marriage; she took over the welfare of women from Artemis, the moon goddess and the protector of young girls. Aphrodite, goddess of love, was the most feminine of the Olympians, very different from the armoured Athena, goddess of war. The gentle Hestia, sister of Zeus, was goddess of the hearth, while Demeter, another sister, was goddess of all plants.

A vase showing some of the deeds of the hero Theseus. Among them are Theseus killing the wild sow of Crommyum, inventing wrestling and, in the centre, killing the legendary Minotaur.

DIFFERENT FORMS

All the Greeks worshipped the same Olympian gods, but they frequently worshipped them in different forms. Artemis, for example, was worshipped at Brauron in Attica as a goddess of hunting and of young women. In Ephesus, however, the same Artemis was the goddess older women prayed to if they wanted to have children. In religion as well as politics, the Greeks kept their independent views.

BROKE AND SORRY

The Greeks did not always take their gods seriously. When the Athenians demanded money from the islanders of Andros, they jokingly told the Andrians that they had to pay because there were two powerful gods in Athens, 'Please' and 'You'd better'. The Andrians replied that their island was so poor that the only gods they had were two who refused to leave, 'Flat broke' and 'Terribly sorry'. In other words, threats were useless, since the islanders had nothing to pay the Athenians with.

In order to please the gods and so win their favour, the Greeks built many impressive temples in their honour, using only the very finest materials. Each temple was believed to be an earthly home for the god or goddess that it was dedicated to.

CAUSING CONFUSION

The Greeks told many stories of how the gods frequently appeared on earth in human form, usually causing trouble in the process. This was especially true of Zeus, since he often fell in love with ordinary women and carried them off, much to the fury of his wife, Hera.

These stories show that the Greek gods were not seen as beings that taught people the difference between right and wrong. They behaved much as humans did - they feasted, they fell in love, and they cheated. Most Greeks did not pray to their gods for goodness, patience and understanding - they prayed for more control over their own lives.

MYSTERY RELIGIONS

There were some cults, however, which were concerned with the more serious issues of life and death and what happened after death. These are called the mystery religions because not much is known about them - their worshippers were sworn to secrecy. The cult of the goddess Demeter and her daughter Persephone, based at Eleusis, was one of the most popular.

Ganymede was the son of the King of Tros who gave his name to Troy. Zeus kidnapped the young boy and made him his own cup-bearer.

TEMPLES AND ORACLES

The Greeks put a lot of time and effort into keeping their gods happy. People prayed to them everywhere, although there were certain places, such as caves or mountain-tops, that were thought to be particularly sacred. Temples were specially-built places of worship - it was believed that the gods used them as their earthly homes.

A HOME FOR A GOD

Temples looked remarkably similar all over the Greek world. They all had the same plan: a main room, or *cella*, where the statue of the god was kept; a smaller room behind, where the sacred vessels and robes were stored; an outer row of graceful columns around the whole building; and a stone altar, placed just outside the entrance to the *cella*. Great care was taken over the proportions of the building - temples like the Parthenon at Athens were built in a way that made every line appear straight to the eye. Decorations included beautifully sculpted friezes and statues, often painted in bright colours. Greek temples were designed to be viewed from the outside; all the rituals, such as the sacrifices to the gods, took place outside, around the altar.

Columns in the Ionic (top) or the Doric (above) styles were used to support the roofs of many of the most magnificent Greek temples.

A man consults the Pythia - the priestess who pronounced the oracles in the temple of Apollo at Delphi. The Pythia made her prophecies after inhaling a special vapour, possibly from the rock cleft over which she sat, to put herself into a magical trance.

PRIESTS AND PRIESTESSES

Priests and priestesses were appointed to make sure that the gods were properly worshipped and that their temples and sacred places were looked after. Their duties varied according to the popularity of the god's cult; priests at famous healing sanctuaries, like that of Aesclepius at Epidauros, often spent all their time arranging accommodation for the many hundreds of visitors. These priests and priestesses were ordinary men and women - they were not specially ordained, as is usual today, and their job was frequently passed down within the family, from one generation to the next. However, all the important decisions about the cult were taken by the government of the city-state, either through its magistrates or through the people's assembly.

A lead tablet with a question for an oracle saying: 'Hermon asks to which god he should pray to have useful children by his wife Kretaia apart from those he already has'.

ORACLES

As well as making sacrifices and performing various rituals to please their gods, the Greeks sometimes consulted them directly for guidance on difficult matters. This was done at the sacred oracle sites, the most famous of which was at Delphi. The oracle at Delphi was consulted by visitors from all over the Greek world and received many treasures from grateful clients. At Delphi, the god Apollo could be questioned through a priestess, called the Pythia, who sat on a three-legged stool over a cleft in the rock. The Pythia was always in a trance when she was consulted, perhaps from fumes rising from the cleft. An enquirer asked her a question and she gave an answer, but the meaning of her answer was usually so obscure that it had to be translated by priests.

A FAMOUS PROPHECY

Delphi issued some very famous prophecies. Once Croesus, the wealthy king of Lydia, consulted it, and asked if he should invade a foreign country. 'If you do,' came the answer, 'you will destroy a great empire.' Unfortunately, Croesus forgot to ask which empire the oracle meant. He invaded the country, suffered defeat, and his own empire was eventually destroyed.

Croesus had done his best to check that the oracle could be trusted. He had sent messengers off to all the oracles in the Greek world to ask them what he, Croesus, was doing on a particular day. On the day in question, Croesus cut up both a tortoise and a lamb with his own hands and boiled them together in a bronze cauldron. The Delphic oracle was the only one to give the right answer.

DICE OR OAK LEAVES?

The oracles that Croesus' messengers consulted used a wide range of methods to foretell the future. Throwing dice or casting lots was an easy method if a person just wanted a yes or no answer. To consult Apollo at Patara in Lycia, people were told to gaze at the surface of a spring. At Dodona in northern Greece, they were instructed to listen out for the voice of the mighty Zeus rustling through the leaves of the oak trees.

A more common way of divining the future was by studying the behaviour of birds. Some birds were closely associated with one particular god - the owl with Athena, for example. There were, obviously, some disbelievers - in one of his plays, *The Birds*, Aristophanes makes fun of his fellow citizens for their faith in oracles and omens. Nevertheless, it was not unusual for even city-state governments to consult the oracles occasionally.

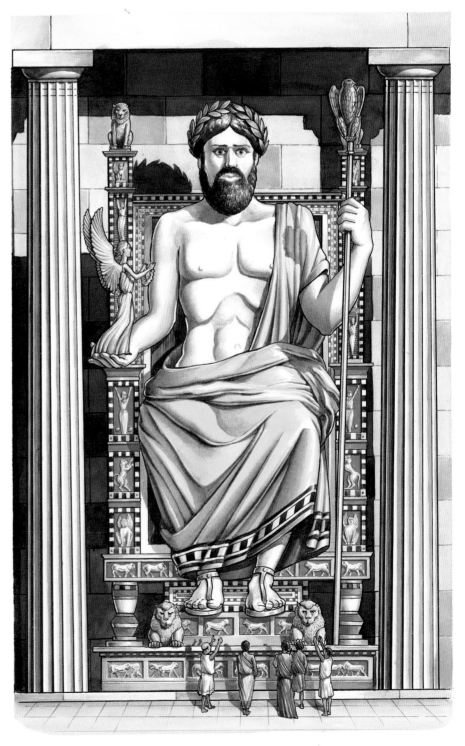

The statue of Zeus, housed in the temple at Olympia, was created by the sculptor Pheidias. One of the Seven Wonders of the World, the figure of the god was 12 metres high, and had ivory skin and golden robes.

DEATH AND BURIAL

The three-headed dog known as Cerberus guarded the entrance of the Underworld to stop living people from wandering in and to keep the souls of the dead from escaping.

The Greeks were not people who were particularly pre-occupied with death - they were much more concerned with living life to the full. They did, though, believe in the soul, and performed various rituals to prepare their dead relatives for their journey to the Underworld - an underground kingdom which they believed to be the final resting place of all mortals.

FUNERAL ARRANGEMENTS

When someone died, their body was first washed and anointed, then dressed in white robes by the women of the family. The body was then put on display for relatives and friends to view.

The next day, before the sun was up, the funeral procession set out to accompany the body to the place of burial. Only close relatives could take part, but women over 60 were excused from this rule, so they often acted as professional mourners, beating their breasts and wailing. As with other Greek processions, all this was accompanied by music.

WANDERING SPIRITS

The tomb was crucially important to the Greeks; without it, the soul of the dead person might be lost for ever. If death was sudden, however, and a tomb was not available, three handfuls of earth thrown over the body were believed to keep the spirit from wandering.

Food and drink, as well as objects used by the dead person, were left inside the tomb. Some tombs have been found with tubes leading from the outside through which more food and drink could be poured later. After the funeral, the family went back home for a special dinner; the period of mourning lasted 30 days.

SPARTAN FUNERALS

Funerals in Sparta were quieter affairs; there was no display of mourning and the body was not embalmed. Burial took place inside the city, so that the young would get used to the sight of death and view it without fear. No objects were buried with the dead person, and the period of mourning was limited to only 11 days.

CROSSING THE RIVER

After burial, the soul was taken by the god Hermes to one of the crossing points between the world of the living and the dead. One of these was believed to be the river Styx in Arcadia. The soul then had to pay a fare of one obol to be transported across the river by the ferryman, Charon - it was therefore customary for living relatives to place a coin in the dead person's mouth before burial.

Aristophanes uses the symbolic crossing of the Styx as a setting in *The Frogs*, one of his comedies. In the play, a chorus of frogs in the river croak as the god Dionysus is ferried across, dressed up as the hero Heracles and pretending to be brave.

THE TRIALS OF DEATH

On the other side of the river, the Underworld was a shadowy place. Most people wandered around aimlessly, although people who had been particularly good during their earthly lives were sometimes sent to the Elysian Fields, a place of great happiness and peace.

Terra-cotta objects found in a girl's grave - a doll seated on a throne, a pair of tiny boots and a thigh-guard (used by women in the preparation of wool).

Those who had been particularly nasty in life were set impossible, never-ending tasks in death. Sisyphus, for example, had to try to roll a heavy stone uphill that kept rolling back on him. Another sinner, Tantalus, had to stand up to his neck in water without ever being able to quench his thirst - every time he stooped to drink, the water level fell out of his reach.

The ruler of this grim realm was Hades, who, according to myth, once carried off Persephone, daughter of the goddess Demeter. Demeter pleaded with Zeus, and Hades was forced to hand Persephone back, but in the meantime she had eaten six pomegranate seeds, which meant she had to stay in the Underworld for six months of the year. The Greeks believed that her return to the world of the living every year brought the spring, and this was one way that they explained the seasons.

A funeral procession makes its noisy way to a tomb outside a Greek town. Musicians play while the professional mourners weep, wail and beat their chests. Relatives carry some of the dead person's possessions to leave in the tomb, as well as oil and honey cake as offerings to the gods.

39

GREEK SHIPS

The sea played a huge part in Greek life, and the steady improvement in the design of ships is the nearest the Greeks came to an interest in technology. The ship was actually the most intricate and essential machine in the ancient world.

This Greek gravestone is decorated with a carving which shows a hoplite sitting on the prow of a trireme.

SHIPS FOR TRADE AND WAR

Merchant ships for carrying goods needed space rather than speed; known as round ships because they were so broad and deep, they were usually sailed rather than rowed. If oars were used at all, it was for manoeuvring or when there was no wind. Warships, though, were rowed - they were light, narrow, and low in the water.

WOODEN WALLS

When the Athenian leader Themistocles persuaded the people of Athens to put the profits from a recently discovered silver mine at Lavrion into the building of a fleet, he may not have realized how crucial that decision was in terms of Greek history. The oracle at Delphi confirmed the wisdom of that decision when attack from the Persians was imminent - the Pythia told the Athenians to 'trust in their wooden walls'.

A mosaic showing a small Greek warship with a long, pointed ram fixed to the prow. The painted eye was supposed to help the ship find its way.

The Athenians interpreted this to mean the 'wooden walls' of their ships, not the fortifications round the Acropolis. They took the oracle's advice, and although they had to watch their city burn, Themistocles promised them: 'We have a city, so long as we have our ships'. At the battle of Salamis in 480 BC, he was proved right.

'The Greeks were like fishermen with a great haul of tunny netted and trapped - stabbing and smashing men with broken oars, pieces of wreckage, whatever came to hand. The sea was filled with screams and groaning, until at last night fell and hid the scene. I could talk for a week and still not tell you all that I saw. But one thing is sure: never before have so many thousands died on a single day.'

— Aeschylus —

TRICKERY AT SEA

Salamis was a significant event in Greek history. The Greeks were probably outnumbered by the Persians by up to three to one, with some 380 ships to the Persians' 1,000. The Greek ships were also slower. However, Themistocles thought up a clever plan. He persuaded the Greeks to take up their positions in the narrow waters between the island of Salamis and the mainland. He tricked the Persians into thinking that the Greeks were going to try to escape through the channel at one end, and so forced the Persians to split their fleet to cover both possible escape routes. When the Persians advanced into the confined waters, their greater speed was of no use - a bloody battle followed, and the Persian fleet was heavily defeated. Two more decisive victories a year later - one by the Greek army at the land battle of Plataea, and another by the navy at Mykale on the coast of Asia Minor - finally put an end to the Persian invasion.

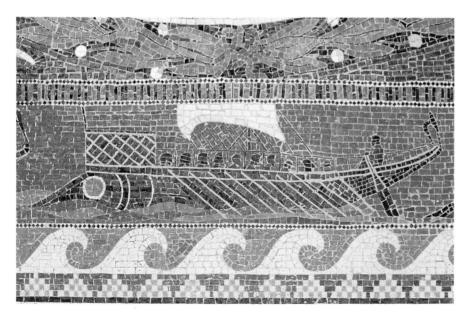

A GREEK TRIREME

1 **Hoplite**
2 **Main deck**
3 **Oarsman**
4 **Oak rib**
5 **Hemp bracing rope**
6 **Stone ballast**
7 **Cypress wood keel**

Built for battle

The prows of Greek warships were shaped like battering-rams. They had a deck on either side from which soldiers could try to board enemy vessels. Warships did have sails, but they were always rowed in battle for maximum manoeuvrability. They were rowed with either 30 oars (triaconters) or 50 oars (penteconters). The Greeks gave them extra power by adding first a second bank of oars (to make biremes), and then a third (triremes). Modern scholars and naval engineers have struggled to find out how the trireme worked. This eventually led to the re-construction of a full-scale Greek trireme, and successful sea trials in the Aegean. A trireme could carry about 200 men; 170 oarsmen, 13 sailors, 10 soldiers and a few officers. The oarsmen were not slaves - they came from the *thetes*, the lowest rank of Athenian society, who could not afford the armour needed to join the army.

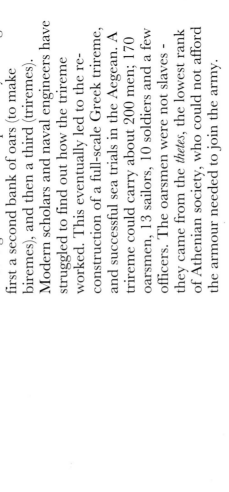

Side view of ship

THE GREEKS AT WAR

Fighting for one's city was considered to be every Greek's patriotic duty. The role that each Greek played in the armed forces was directly related to his social position. Rich men who could afford a horse joined the cavalry; those that had enough money to buy armour became hoplites, heavily-armoured soldiers. Poorer people served as lightly-armed archers or stone-slingers.

HOPLITES

The hoplites were the key fighting force in an ancient Greek army. Their *hopla*, or 'arms', consisted of a long spear for stabbing, a short sword, a helmet with a suitably fearsome crest and a round, heavy shield. Hoplites fought in a formation known as a *phalanx*, made up of several lines of men. Their main tactic was to keep their front line unbroken; the enemy was then faced with a wall of shields locked together, bristling with long spears. Hoplites needed a lot of training to be able to fight in such a disciplined way.

The fighting itself resembled a rugby scrum, and once a line had broken, individual soldiers could easily be picked off. This explains the great difference in casualty figures on the two sides in hoplite battles. The side which did not hold its line usually lost many men, while the other side escaped very lightly. This style of warfare meant that each man had to rely on the courage of his neighbours, in the same way that he relied on their good sense when it came to running the city. Greek warfare may have had a lot to do with the character of Greek political life.

UNEXPECTED VICTORY

The first great test for hoplite warfare came when Persia invaded Greece. At the battle of Marathon in 490 BC, the Athenian army roundly defeated the Persians, and this gave it a new self-confidence.

Armed only with a sword and without a saddle or stirrups, a horseman could not fight effectively against heavily armoured foot soldiers protected by spears.

This important victory was celebrated by many Greek writers. The historian Herodotus describes Marathon as the first time a Greek army charged at a run. In his epitaph, the poet Aeschylus said that he only wanted to be remembered as one who had fought in the infantry at Marathon.

VICTORY IN DEFEAT

The Spartan defeat by the Persians at Thermopylae in 480 BC ranks with the Athenian victory at Marathon in importance. The Spartans threw back wave after wave of the Persians by their brilliant tactics; sometimes they turned their backs and pretended to run for their lives, only to turn fiercely on the Persians when they charged after them. The Spartans' eventual defeat was almost inevitable, as they were vastly outnumbered, but their brave and brilliant fighting only added to their fearsome reputation.

This relief shows the goddess Athena mourning for Athenian warriors who have been killed in battle.

GREEKS AGAINST GREEKS

All this bravery came to a bitter end in the Peloponnesian War (431-404 BC), when Athens and Sparta, with their various allies, turned their forces against each other. The war boasted no great battles; the Athenians had a better navy than the Spartans, but a weaker army. Athens suffered a series of setbacks, including a devastating plague which broke out in the city in 430 BC, killing a quarter of the population. She was finally defeated in 404 BC, but only after Sparta built its own fleet using Persian money.

Wars between the various city-states continued, however, a constant drain on manpower and resources. Thus the Greeks were unprepared for the threat of a new power that was taking shape in the north.

The Spartans held the narrow pass of Thermopylae against 250,000 Persians for two days. Finally, the Persians surrounded the 300 Spartans who fought with broken swords and even hands and teeth until they were overwhelmed.

MARVELS IN MACEDONIA

Just as hoplite fighting had brought the great age of Greece into being, so its eclipse brought the age to an end. To the north in Macedonia, a new kind of army was training. These infantry were armed with spears about 5 m long, designed to break the hoplite wall before the hoplite spears could even reach them. It took a lot of practice, but King Philip of Macedonia and his son Alexander were determined men. The great age of Greece was passing.

GREECE AFTER THE GREEKS

This Roman mosaic, found in the ruins of Pompeii, shows Alexander the Great riding his famous horse Bucephalus at the Battle of Issus in 333 BC.

After the fourth century BC, Greece lost its political independence to the Macedonians. But the spread of Greek culture had hardly even begun. In the period of its political decline, Greece was to have more impact on Europe and the Near East than it did when it was at the height of its power.

ALEXANDER THE GREAT

Alexander the Great was the son of Philip of Macedonia, a skilled and ambitious general who conquered the Greek world as the power of the city-states began to crumble. Philip very much admired the culture of the Greek people and wanted his son to be brought up in the Greek tradition. Alexander was educated by the philosopher Aristotle, and the boy grew up inspired by tales of the Greek heroes.

When Alexander became king of Macedonia at the age of only 20, he was determined to expand his empire further. After first stamping out rebellion in the Greek states, Alexander began a series of brilliant military campaigns in which he conquered most of the then known world and spread Greek culture and the Greek language as far as India.

He first attacked Persia, where his army defeated King Darius's forces at the battle of Issus in 333 BC. Alexander next marched south and laid siege first to the city of Tyre and then to Gaza. His army moved on from there to invade and conquer Egypt, where Alexander was hailed as the son of the god Amon.

Returning from Egypt, he marched east into Asia. At Gaugamela, a second victory against the Persians finally sealed the fate of the Persian empire - the city of Babylon surrendered, and the rich cities of Susa and Persepolis were quickly captured.

Alexander continued on into Parthia, then east again through Bactria and lastly to India, where he defeated the forces of King Porus.

In several places along the way, Alexander ordered cities to be built in his honour. These were all named Alexandria, and were often modelled on Greek cities - most had a temple, a *gymnasium*, and inscriptions on their various public buildings taken from the Greek philosophers.

Alexander's empire stretched from Greece to India with Babylon as its capital. He was one of the greatest generals who ever lived. His well-trained army smashed the Persian army and ended the reign of their king, Darius III.

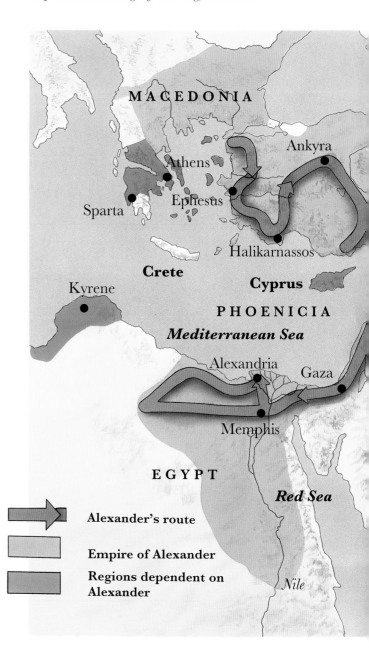

MACEDONIA

Athens

Sparta   Ephesus

Ankyra

Halikarnassos

Crete   Cyprus

Kyrene

PHOENICIA

Mediterranean Sea

Alexandria   Gaza

Memphis

EGYPT

Red Sea

Nile

➡ **Alexander's route**

Empire of Alexander

Regions dependent on Alexander

DEATH OF A KING

Alexander had even more ambitious plans, including an expedition to conquer Arabia. But at the age of 33, he was taken ill with malaria and died. His body was taken to Egypt - first to Memphis and then to Alexandria, where it was placed in a beautiful, richly decorated tomb.

After his death, Alexander's empire was too vast to survive as a single entity. It eventually split up into several kingdoms, but all of these continued to be strongly influenced by Greek ideas.

During all this period, Rome had been little more than a village. Its power did not reach the eastern Mediterranean until some 200 years after Alexander.

A ROMAN PROVINCE

When the mighty Roman armies swept through Greece in the 140s BC, the country became a province of the Roman empire. Culturally, however, the spirit of Greece lived on. Roman sculpture, painting and literature were almost totally dependent on Greek models. Virgil's great epic poem, the *Aeneid*, for example, tells a story of a hero fleeing from Troy, just as Homer's hero Odysseus had done. But perhaps the greatest legacy of the Greeks to us today is the New Testament - when Christianity spread through the Roman empire in the first few centuries AD, Greek was one of the first languages used to write down the new teachings.

The magnificent Christian art of the eastern Roman empire drew heavily on Greek styles.

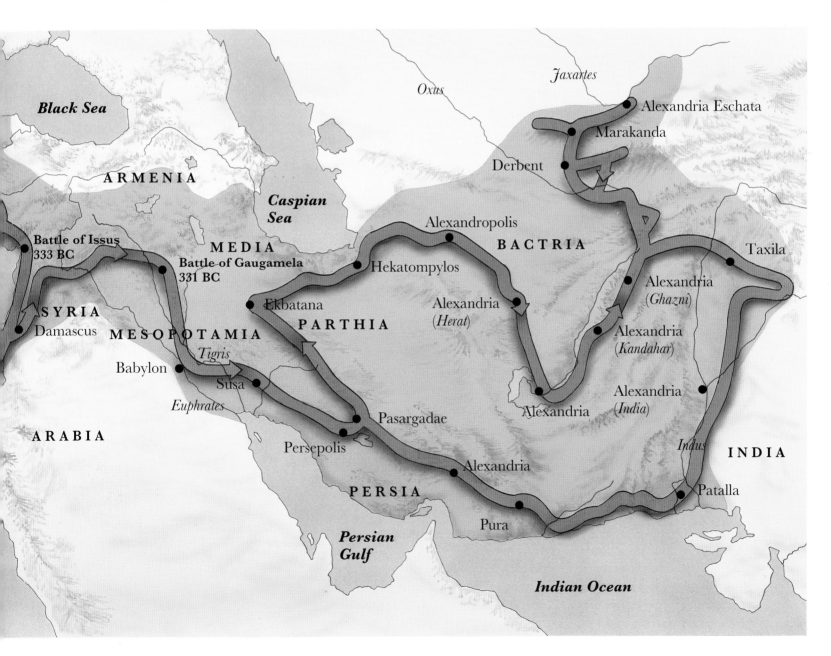

Black Sea

Oxus

Jaxartes

Alexandria Eschata

Marakanda

Derbent

ARMENIA

Caspian Sea

Alexandropolis

BACTRIA

Taxila

Battle of Issus 333 BC

MEDIA

Battle of Gaugamela 331 BC

Hekatompylos

Alexandria (*Ghazni*)

SYRIA

Ekbatana

PARTHIA

Alexandria (*Herat*)

Alexandria (*Kandahar*)

Damascus

MESOPOTAMIA

Tigris

Babylon

Susa

Euphrates

Pasargadae

Alexandria

Alexandria (*India*)

ARABIA

Persepolis

Indus

INDIA

Alexandria

Patalla

PERSIA

Pura

Persian Gulf

Indian Ocean

KEY DATES AND GLOSSARY

Early Greek Cultures c.3000-800 BC

3000-1450 The Minoan civilization discovers bronze by combining copper with tin, resulting in what we call the 'Bronze Age'; other civilizations had also discovered the metal by this time

2000 The Minoans begin to use hieroglyphs, a form of picture writing

1900-1400 Minoans build Knossos Palace, centre of power, in Crete

1450 Volcanic eruption at Thera destroys Minoan civilization; Mycenaeans from Greece take over Knossos

1400 Mycenaeans become a great power

1250 Siege of Troy by Mycenaean kings; slow decline of Mycenaean power

1100-800 The Dark Ages

The Archaic Period c.800-500 BC

800 Greeks develop the most advanced form of writing; Homer probably wrote his epic poems at this time

776 First Olympic Games held

550 City of Sparta founded

508 First Democratic Government established in Athens

490 Persians attempt invasion of Greece; defeated at battle of Marathon

480 The naval battle of Salamis, in which the Persian fleet is defeated

479 The battle of Plataea, in which the Greeks defeat the Persians; at the same time, the Persian fleet is destroyed at Mykale, Asia Minor, so ending the Persian invasion

The Classical Age c.500-336 BC

443-429 The age of Pericles - Athens reaches the height of its power

431-404 Peloponnesian War between Sparta and Athens, won by Sparta

387 Plato founds a philosophical school in Athens, and begins to write his great philosophical works

354 Xenophon, Greek historian, is born

The Hellenistic Period c.337-146 BC

336 Alexander the Great becomes King of Macedonia and begins his victorious 11-year campaign against the Persians

336-330 Alexander's wide conquests create the Hellenistic World, a period of Greek influence and power, which survives until long after his death

333 Battle of Issus, in which Alexander defeats Persia

Three scenes from Homer's Odyssey, *one of the most famous of ancient Greek epics. In the first (left) Odysseus and his crew blind the one-eyed, man-eating Cyclops in order to escape from his clutches. In the second (centre), protected by a magic charm himself, Odysseus forces the witch Circe to break the spell that has transformed his crew into swine.*

332 Alexander conquers Egypt
331 Alexander defeats the Persians at the battle of Gaugamela and becomes King of Persia
323 Alexander the Great dies
323-322 Lamian War, between the Greeks and the Macedonians, in which the Greeks are defeated. Greece is governed from Macedonia
168 Macedonia is defeated by the Romans, and is placed under Roman rule along with Greece
146 Greece becomes part of the Roman Empire

Glossary

agora: a large, open space in a Greek city, used for markets and public meetings

amphora: a jar with two handles, used for storing both liquids (mainly wine, water and oil) and some foodstuffs

andron: the men's quarters of a Greek house, where parties were held

assembly: the main governing body in a Greek democracy. All citizens were entitled to attend

boulé: the council that drafted the laws passed by the assembly, and prepared the agendas for assembly meetings. It was made up of 500 men chosen by lot, 50 from each of the 10 tribes of Athens

citizen: an adult, native-born, male member of a Greek city-state

democracy: a state or country which is ruled by its people. Greek cities were small enough to enable all of their citizens to attend the government assembly

gynaikon: the women's quarters in a Greek house

hetaira: a woman who entertained at parties by singing, dancing, and talking

helot: a Spartan slave; helots were carefully controlled by their masters, who were constantly prepared for war and rebellion

hoplite: a heavily-armoured soldier who fought on foot

ostracism: the system by which people could vote against a member of the assembly by writing his name on a piece of pottery called an *ostrakon*. If over 6,000 people voted against someone, that person was banished from the city for ten years

phalanx: a solid body of men that formed an almost invincible wall of shields and bristling spears against attackers

polis: a Greek city-state. Each *polis* had its own government

prytany: the executive committee of the *boulé* or council, made up of 50 men from one of the 10 tribes of Athens

tholos: the round building near the *agora* in which members of the prytany met, ate and even slept

trireme: a warship which the Greeks strengthened by adding two extra banks of oars, requiring 170 oarsmen, and carrying a total of 200 men

In the final scene (right), Odysseus listens to the haunting songs of the Sirens, sung to bewitch all passing mortals and lure them to their doom. He has protected his crew by plugging their ears with beeswax - the hero himself is lashed to the ship's mast so that he cannot act while under the Sirens' spell and force his crew to row towards their lair.

47

INDEX